Charlie the Fish
Surrounded by Love

Written & Illustrated by Darla Prether

High Note
Publishing

CHARLIE THE FISH
Surrounded by Love

© 2020 by Darla Prether, all rights reserved.
No portion of this book may be reproduced in any form without the written permission of the author and publisher, except for brief quotations in reviews.

Books may be purchased through Amazon or by contacting the author.

Publisher: High Note Publishing

ISBN: 978-1-7357521-0-5

Printed in the U.S.A.

*To my husband Craig,
who not only modeled for God's hands in the book,
but has also been the hands and heart
of God in my life.*

Contents

Charlie 1

Best Friends 4

Where Are You? 11

Charlie's New Friend 13

Down, Down, Down 17

God's Jealousy 20

Love's Mission 22

Regrets 26

Hope 29

Just in Time 34

Delivery 40

All Mine 42

A New Song 44

CHARLIE

This is Charlie.
He is a friendly fish that lives
happily at the edge of the sea,
near a small embankment.

Charlie's happiness is due to
what is on the other side of the bank.

On the other side of the bank is the Great Wood. It is a captivating wood where the trees are tall and majestic, and their leaves glisten as the gentle breeze and sunshine play a duet. If Charlie listens carefully, and remains still long enough, he can hear the soothing sounds of a delightful melody.

God lives in this beautiful wood, but he often comes to the water's edge to visit Charlie. He is quite fond of this little creature he created, and he loves him dearly. He enjoys Charlie's company so much that he takes daily walks to visit him.

BEST FRIENDS

One morning God followed his usual path out to the sea. Charlie could feel the increasing vibrations in the water with each step. "He's coming! He's coming!" Charlie quickly swam to the bank to meet him.

As God reached the embankment by the sea, he saw Charlie's little yellow face peeking out of the water, expressing sheer delight. God said with a chuckle, "I see you, Little One!"

As he so often did, God lay over the embankment with his arms draped into the water, cupping his hands to gently sustain his little friend. Charlie swam between his fingers and settled comfortably in God's hands.

The hours flew by as they enjoyed each other's company. God playfully created small waves with his hand so that Charlie could do somersaults. They laughed and laughed at all the bubbles! They chatted about *this*, and they chatted about *that*, until words were no longer necessary.

So they sat. They were happy just to be together.

They sat and watched what seemed to be a silent movie in the heavens. A large cloud drifted along in the wind and began to form a fluffy, round sheep.

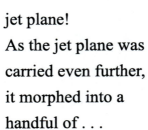

jet plane!
As the jet plane was carried even further, it morphed into a handful of . . .

balloons!
As the wind carried the balloons along, they waved "goodbye!" and the clouds gradually dispersed.

As the sheep was carried further by the wind, it gradually became a . . .

Charlie drifted off to a peaceful sleep in the palm of God's hand, as if he had been told a bedtime story. God tenderly placed him back into his home in the water, and tiptoed back to the Great Wood.

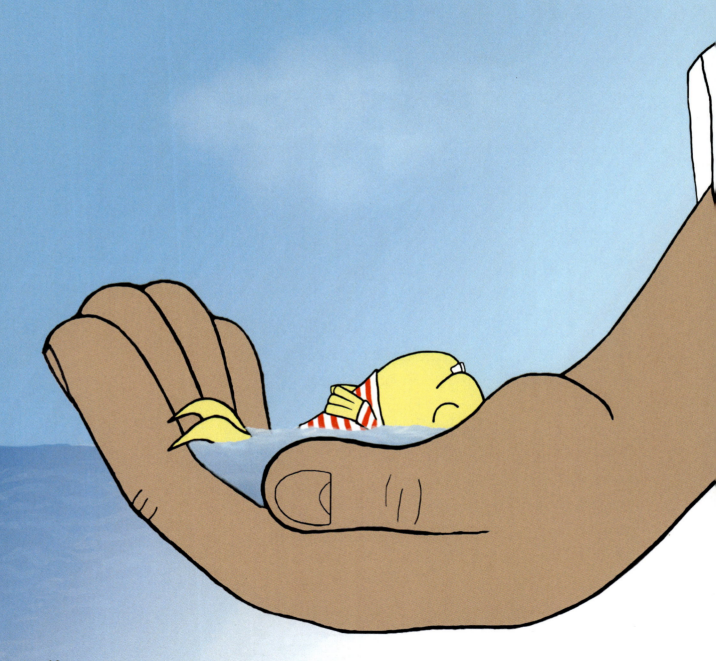

WHERE ARE YOU?

The next day, God was filled with excitement and anticipation to see Charlie again. As he began to follow his path out to the sea, God could see the embankment in the distance. He stretched his neck to try to catch a glimpse of that little yellow face.

As he got closer, God expected Charlie to pop his head up to yell, "Surprise!" But no little face appeared. God leaned over the water, waiting for Charlie to emerge, but he didn't. God walked back and forth along the water's edge, calling to Charlie, "Little One! Where are you, Little One?" Charlie was nowhere to be seen. Heartbroken, God collapsed to his knees by the water, well aware of what had happened to his little friend.

2956 S
0004603

00046032956

Inspected By: Yesica_Zepeda

Sell your books at sellbackyourBook.com!
Go to sellbackyourBook.com and get an instant price quote. We even pay the shipping - see what your old books are worth today!

Sell your books at
sellbackyourBook.com!
Go to sellbackyourBook.com
and get an instant price
quote. We even pay the
shipping - see what your old
books are worth today!

Inspected By: Jessica_Zepeda

00046035956

CHARLIE'S NEW FRIEND

The night before, after God had placed Charlie back into his home in the water, Charlie decided to go for a midnight swim to grab a snack.

As Charlie swam along in the moonlight, a small gray creature resembling clay approached him. "Hi, I'm Barnie." Charlie strained to see who was talking to him. For such a big voice, the critter was so small! Charlie introduced himself to the little creature and chatted for a while. Charlie took a liking to Barnie, and they became new friends.

"You look like a great swimmer and seem so strong," said Barnie. "Could you take me for a ride around the sea?"

Flattered, Charlie quickly complied. He continued on with his swim, this time carrying Barnie on his side.

Soon after, they came across another clay-like creature. "Hey, Barnie! That looks like *you*!" said Charlie.

"It's my sister, Bernice," said Barnie. "Can she have a ride too?"

Charlie again complied, eager to please his new friend.

A little while later, they came across another relative, this time Barnie's cousin, who also wanted a ride. Charlie continued on, meeting family member after family member. Brothers, sisters, aunts, uncles... boy did Barnie have a big family! One by one, each member of the family hitched a ride, attaching itself to Charlie.

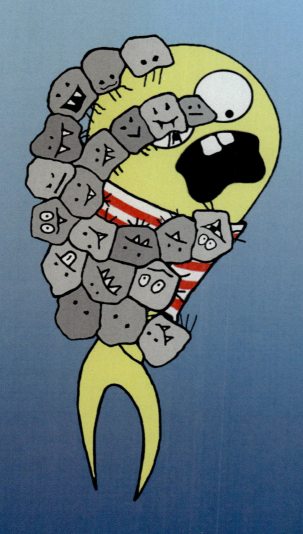

DOWN, DOWN, DOWN

The weight had increased so gradually that Charlie didn't realize how heavy his passengers had become. He struggled to swim and tried with all his might to propel himself forward. Charlie felt himself being pulled downward, like he was being sucked by a vacuum. Down he plummeted, sinking further and further down to the very depths of the sea.

He landed on the ocean floor with a thud, creating a cloud of debris. Even after the dust cleared, very little of Charlie's beautiful yellow skin was visible. Instead, he looked like a sunken ship encrusted with barnacles. Covered with creatures, Charlie could no longer move. Every breath was a struggle due to the weight on his gills. Charlie tried to open his eyes, but they were covered with creatures. He strained to hear, but the piercing chatter drowned out all other sounds.

The bottom of the dark ocean was extremely cold. But Charlie found comfort and warmth from the blanket of gray creatures. Barnie whispered eerily in his ear, "We'll keep you warm. We're your friends." The clay-like family settled into their new home. Under their influence, a feeling of sluggishness came over Charlie, and he drifted off to sleep. He slept day after day and night after night.

Entombed at the bottom of the sea, Charlie failed to hear the once familiar voice crying out from the water's edge. God moaned: "Little One... Little One! Come back to me, Little One!"

GOD'S JEALOUSY

God knew that Charlie had been taken from him, and he burned with jealousy. As time passed, God's desire to be reunited with Charlie increased.

He continued his daily walks from the Great Wood to the edge of the sea, but with each passing day God stepped up the pace.

As his desire grew to see Charlie, the heat that indwelled God also intensified. As he stood daily at the water's edge, life in the sea began to stir as the environment became increasingly heated. There came an upsurge in activity as some of them became uncomfortable with the heat, and others were stimulated by it.

LOVE'S MISSION

As God's jealousy burned, Love for Charlie permeated the waters. In the middle of the sea, far from the water's edge, a whale swimming on the surface was suddenly roused by Love.

She leapt out of the water, twirling around like a ballet dancer, and slapped the water on her way back down.

As if assigned to a mission, the whale torpedoed down toward the ocean floor to where Charlie lay sleeping. In one fell swoop the whale scooped up Charlie in her mouth and began her ascent to the top.

Nauseated by the clay-like creatures, the whale ejected Barnie's family one by one, leaving a trail of gray creatures spinning dizzily behind. They would move on to find another victim to ensnare.

REGRETS

The whale rose to the water's surface and, with a portion of her back exposed, floated there motionless.

Deep inside the whale, curled up in a little ball, Charlie gradually stirred from his slumber. He opened his eyes slowly and blinked a few times but only saw darkness. He listened carefully but was surrounded by silence.

While he was bruised and weakened, at least he was free from the intoxicating grip of the clay-like creatures and could think more clearly. Charlie realized that Barnie's family had tricked him. He should have never agreed to give them a ride.

HOPE

Feeling like he was locked in a prison cell, Charlie lay inside the whale for many days and nights. It was uncomfortably hot and stuffy, and he longed for a breath of fresh air.

From the depths of the fish Charlie called out for help.

His cries seemed to be answered as he drifted off to sleep and floated into a dream. His dream took him home to where God held him in the palm of his hand. There they played together and made bubbles, laughing until their sides hurt. They talked heart to heart, as best friends do, and then rested in silence, falling into a peaceful sleep.

As soon as Charlie fell asleep in his dream, however, he awoke to reality. After feeling so close to Love in his dream, Charlie's heart was ignited and he longed to see his best friend again. He decided that if he ever got out of this predicament, he would never go his own way again but would stay close to God no matter what.

As Charlie lay there in the dark, Love embraced him and gave him hope.

JUST IN TIME

After some time had passed, God emerged from the Great Wood and followed his path out to the sea. By this point he burned with such intense jealousy that with every step of his feet the dry grass smoldered. Filled with determination, God shot out to the embankment like a rocket.

As he reached the water's edge, the water began to simmer and swirl. From the very depths of his being, God exploded: "Come back to me, Little One! Come back!" His voice thunderously echoed across the sky, and the entire sea trembled at his words.

Feeling vibrations from inside the whale, Charlie sat up suddenly. The whale was once again roused by Love and began to stir. Charlie sat in the darkness with his eyes as big as saucers wondering, "Could it be?" A light appeared to illuminate the darkness as Charlie realized what was happening. He cried out, "He's coming! He's coming!" As the words rolled off his tongue, his heart leapt with joy.

Invigorated by Love, the whale snorted and sprayed showers into the air.

The sun illuminated the water, forming a beautiful rainbow above the whale. The whale looked up, puckered her lips and spewed Charlie out, catapulting him high into the air. Charlie gasped for breath as he quickly ascended into the rainbow.

He landed on top of the fountain where the water washed over him.

DELIVERY

Suddenly, Charlie was caught by the wind and carried away. As he soared through the air the thought came to him, "Don't look down." So he kept his eyes fixed straight ahead. He knew that God was drawing him back to himself. Love was in the wind and carried Charlie across the sea to his destination. Approaching the seashore, Charlie could see God's big face beaming with delight.

As if delivering precious cargo, the wind gently lowered Charlie into God's outstretched hand.

ALL MINE

God tenderly took Charlie's fragile body and whispered, "You're *mine*, Little One, *all mine*." He pulled Charlie close to his face and breathed his breath into him.

Charlie felt the renewed life surge through him. His yellow skin glowed like the sun, and he felt a warm energy pulsating through his body, with Love permeating his being.

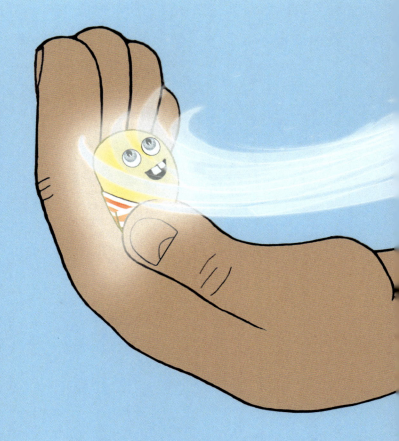

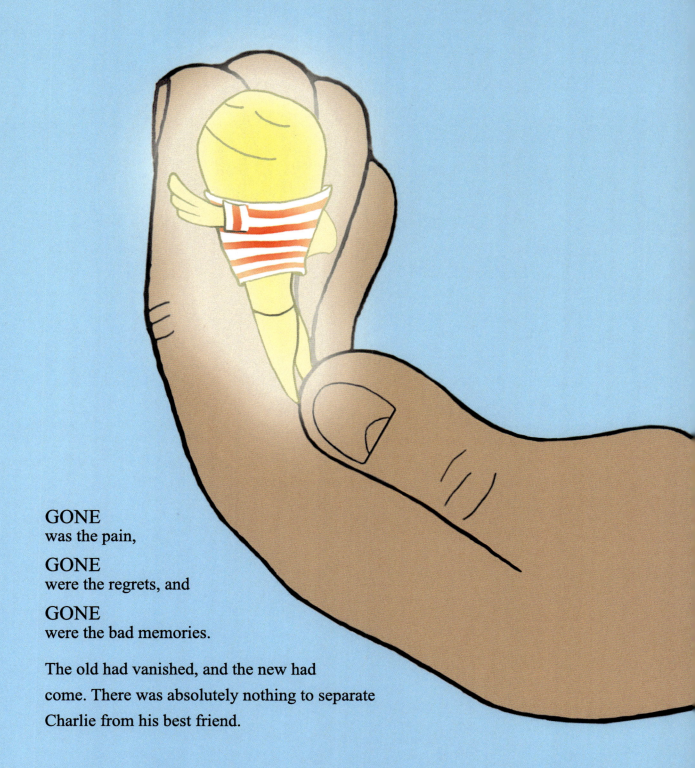

GONE
was the pain,

GONE
were the regrets, and

GONE
were the bad memories.

The old had vanished, and the new had come. There was absolutely nothing to separate Charlie from his best friend.

A NEW SONG

Completely satisfied, God began to sing out joyfully. It was a new song, and a catchy one at that. As God sang, the delightful melody washed over Charlie and he couldn't help but burst forth in harmony. Love was in the song, and their duet absolutely soared.

A renewed bond had formed between the two, one that would never be broken, no matter what. So they sang the New Song at the top of their lungs... the song that had no end.

THE ~~END~~ BEGINNING

Made in the USA
Monee, IL
19 February 2021